WALKS ARO… E CAVE… MEN… …ILLS

by

Dr. Andrew R. Farrant
(University of Bristol
Spelaeological Society)

A guide to walks illustrating the karst landforms and some accessible caves within the Mendip Hills

British Cave Research Association
Cave Studies Series Number 8
1999

CONTENTS

Acknowledgements
Thanks must go to Graham Mullan for the final editing and typesetting, as well as for providing information on some of the sites and to Mike Simms who provided much help and advice. Steve Cottle, Pete Glanville, Chris Howes and Pat Farrant kindly provided the photographs. Thanks also to Katy Booth for the use of her computer. This book is dedicated to Bryan Ellis, the Series Editor, who passed away shortly before it was completed.

Front cover photograph: Cheddar Gorge, © Cheddar Showcaves Ltd
Back cover photograph: The Witches Kitchen, Wookey Hole, © Wookey Hole Caves Ltd

WARNING
The author and the British Cave Research Association strongly advise readers of this guide against entering any caves unless in the company of an experienced caver. Exceptions are offered by the show caves at Wookey Hole and Cheddar. Many of the sites are on private land and the wishes of the landowners and tenants must be respected.
Mention in this guide does not imply a public right of way.

ISBN 0 900265 21 3

THE CAVES AND KARST OF THE AREA

Although a relatively compact area, the Mendip Hills contain a wide variety of both rock types and landforms. In particular, it is the action of water on the limestone which adds so much character to the Mendip landscape. The soluble nature of the limestone gives rise to the suite of landforms known as 'karst'; characterised by underground drainage routes through caves, stream sinks, springs, dry valleys and gorges. On Mendip, the distinctive feel of the landscape is enhanced by the marked contrast between the flat alluvial Somerset Levels to the south, the bleak rugged upstanding limestone plateau with its dry valleys and gorges and the heather clad sandstone summits such as Blackdown and North Hill. In winter, when fog masks the flat alluvial levels, Mendip, rising up out of the mist, seems to become a separate world of its own. This guide is intended to highlight and explain some of the lesser known karst features in the area, as well as providing more information on the better known tourist sites through a series of excursions.

The Mendip Hills lie 20 km south of Bristol and extend for some 50 km from the coast at Weston-super-Mare, inland to Frome in the east. Geologically they consist of a series of four en-echelon anticlines each with a central core of Devonian Old Red Sandstone flanked by Carboniferous Limestone. Although laterally extensive, the Mendips are often no more than 10 km across. In the west, the hills are bordered to the north and south by recently drained flat alluvial plains, known locally as 'Levels'. Here the hills form a very distinct topographic unit rising steeply from sea-level to a flat plateau around 200-250 m. Further inland, the hills become more subdued until at Frome they merge into the surrounding landscape and the Carboniferous Limestone is buried beneath a cover of younger rocks. Topographically the highest points occur on the Old Red Sandstone in the core of the anticlines, reaching a maximum elevation of 325 m on Blackdown.

Most of the modern drainage is underground, the exceptions being on the impermeable Old Red Sandstone, the younger cover rocks and in some of the valleys in the extreme west and east of the Mendips. Most of the surrounding rivers drain west to the Bristol Channel, except in the far east where the drainage pattern is orientated to the north-east. Rainfall is high, exceeding 1000 mm on the plateau and the prevailing winds are from the south-west. Unlike all of the other major karst areas in Britain, the Mendips lay beyond the southern limits of the known Pleistocene glacial advances during the last million years or so. Thus, there are none of the bare rock pavements or glacially scoured 'U' shaped valleys that are so characteristic of the Yorkshire Dales and South Wales karst areas.

Although not a wild or remote area, a good map is essential for route finding. The Ordnance Survey produce two very good 1:25,000 Explorer Maps (Sheets 141 & 142) covering the entire Mendip area and much of the Somerset Levels to the south. All of the excursions are fairly short and can be covered by a reasonably fit person in less than half a day. Several of the excursions overlap and so can be amalgamated or altered to suit individual taste or requirements.

Geology of the Region

Karst features are primarily developed on the Carboniferous Limestone, although the Triassic Dolomitic Conglomerate and some of the Jurassic limestones also exhibit karstic landforms and caves. The distinctive Mendip style of karst landscape owes much to its long and intricate geological history. Figure 2 provides the general stratigraphy of the area.

The oldest rocks known in the area are the Silurian andesitic lavas, tuffs (ash) and shales which are exposed along the crest of Beacon Hill, north of Shepton Mallet. Although limited in outcrop, they have been extensively quarried for roadstone. Lying above the Silurian rocks is the Devonian Old Red Sandstone, comprising over 450 m of red and brown mudstones, sandstones and conglomerates. These were deposited on an alluvial plain by large, probably braided, rivers under arid conditions some 350 million years ago. Marine limestones of the same age around Torquay indicate that the contemporary shoreline lay nearby to the south.

Succeeding the Devonian sandstone is a sequence of shales and muddy limestones, the Lower Limestone Shales, marking the transition from terrestrial fluvial sedimentation to shallow marine deposits as the sea encroached north. This marine transgression eventually led to the deposition of the Carboniferous Limestone about 340 to 300 million years ago. As the sea gradually cleared, the limestone was deposited in a shallow marine environment situated just to the south of a major landmass, with deeper water offshore to the south. At the time the area lay close to the Equator and the climate was warm. Few rivers drained the landmass to the north, known as St. George's Land, so the limestone was uncontaminated by land derived sediment and consequently is generally pure and massively bedded.

The limestone sequence, which totals over a kilometre in thickness, can be sub-divided into a number of units; the oldest being the Black Rock Limestone, a dark grey bioclastic limestone (formed of many broken fossil fragments) with abundant crinoid debris, brachiopods and some corals. This is probably the most familiar limestone to cavers as the majority of the swallet caves are developed within this unit. Above this lies the Burrington Oolite, a very pure, pale oolitic limestone, overlain by the much finer dark grey mudstones of the Clifton Down Limestone which are often locally packed with large brachiopods and Lithostrotian coral colonies. At the top of the sequence is the Hotwells Limestone, a thick series of bioclastic limestones, often quite fossiliferous.

Limestone deposition was curtailed at the end of the Lower Carboniferous by a massive influx of land derived sediment, which produced the Quartzitic Sandstone. This sandstone, deposited by a series of large river deltas, heralded the start of the Middle and Upper Carboniferous, a period dominated by the laying down of the Coal Measures. These are a thick series of deltaic sandstone and shales with coal seams, which outcrop primarily to the north of the Mendips in the Somerset Coalfield, but can be found in a small inlier at Ebbor Gorge.

Following the deposition of the Coal Measures, a major period of uplift and erosion occurred about 280 million years ago. This was the result of the collision of earlier continents to form a vast 'super-continent' called Pangea. The Variscan Orogeny as this mountain building period is termed, had a profound effect. The Palaeozoic rocks were folded into the four asymmetric en-echelon periclines (Blackdown, North Hill, Pen Hill and Beacon Hill), mentioned above. On the northern side of these periclines, the rocks dip steeply to the north at around 50-70°. In places such as at Churchill Rocks, this folding was severe enough to overturn the strata, forming a 'nappe' structure. To the south the dip is usually less at around 20-30°. A schematic cross section through the Blackdown

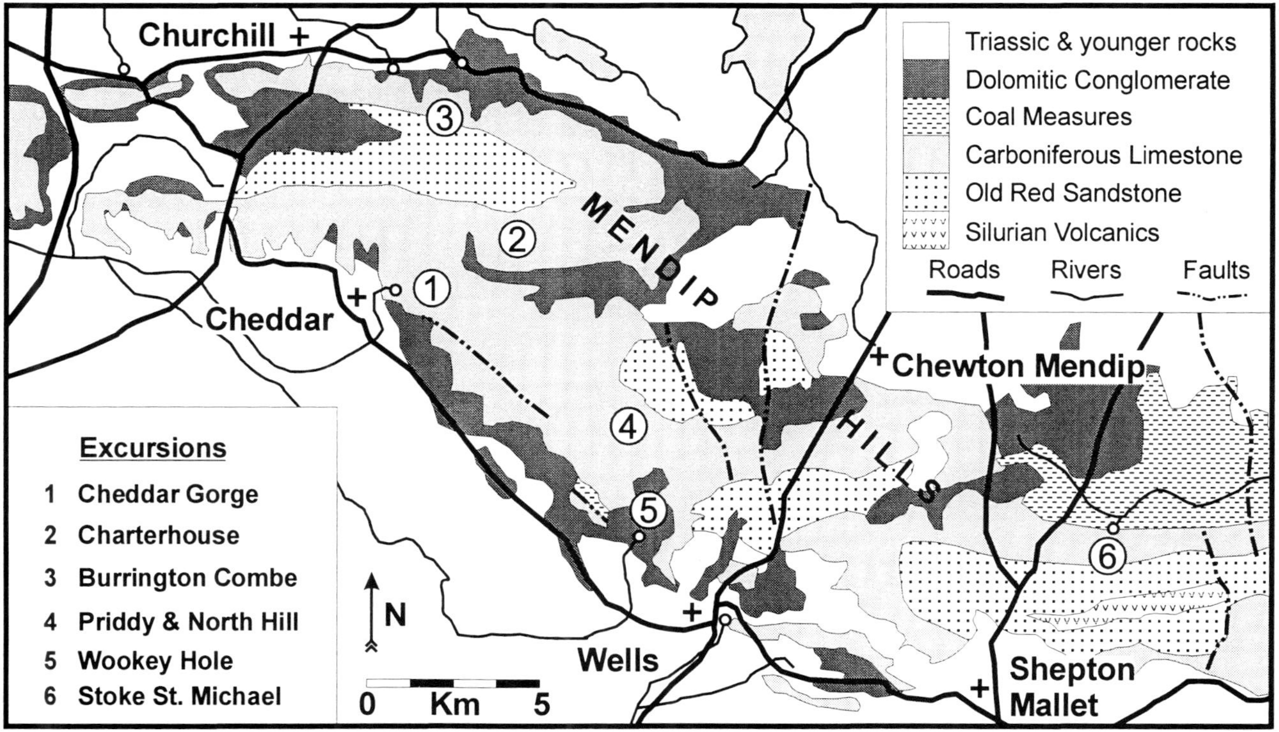

Simplified geological map of the Mendip Hills, showing the location of excursions described.

pericline is shown on Figure 3. Many of the faults on Mendip were also initiated at this time. These can be divided into two groups; a major series of east-west thrust faults, such as the Southern Overthrust and the Ebbor Thrust fault, and a series of north-south faults such as the Biddle and Stock Hill Faults. Reactivation of these faults has occurred several times during the subsequent 280 million years.

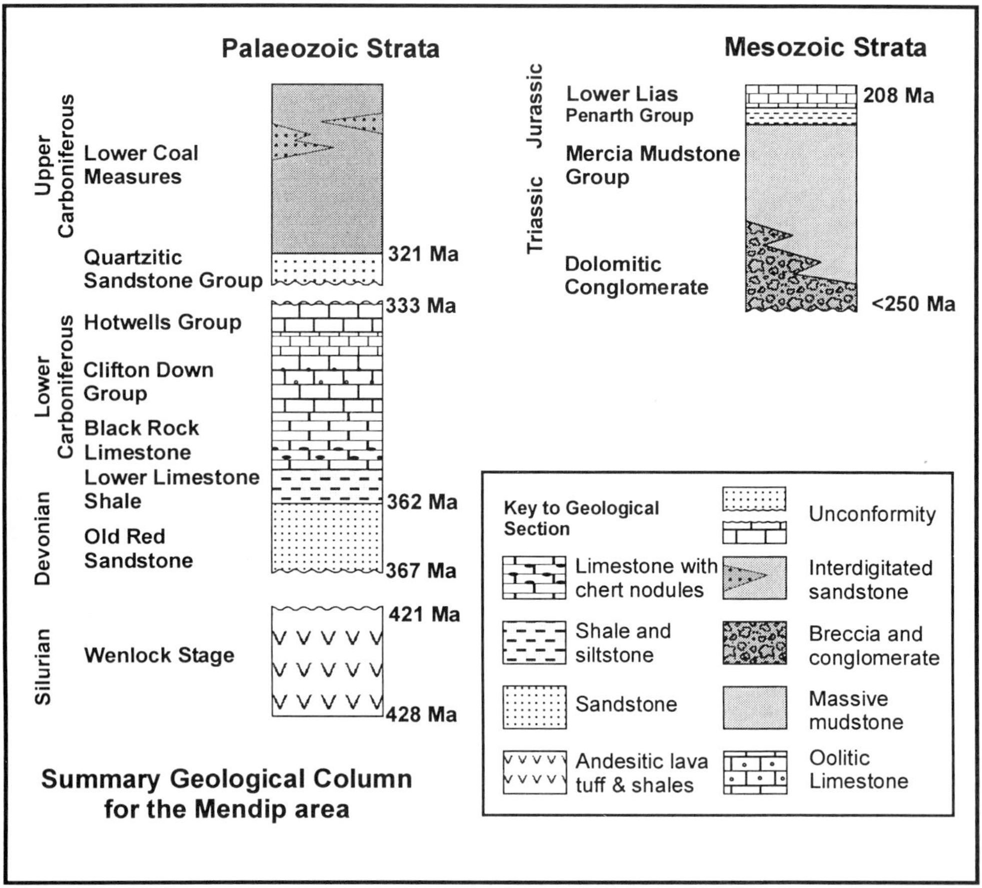

General geological stratigraphy of the Mendips.

Thus the Mendips first became a range of steep rugged mountains some 280 million years ago. During this sub-aerial phase, which lasted some 80 million years, many hundreds of metres of rock were eroded away. Geological evidence suggests that the Mendips were reduced to near their present topographic level during this time. During the Triassic, the climate was hot and dry, with occasional storms and many deep steep sided ravines or 'wadis' were incised into the flanks of the hills. These subsequently became infilled with a breccia of limestone and sandstone pebbles cemented by calcite to form the

Dolomitic Conglomerate. These marginal deposits thin rapidly away from the Mendips, laterally grading into red mudstones known as the Mercia Mudstone which often contain evaporite minerals indicative of a hot dry climate. However, there was enough water to form caves and some of these now infilled passages and fissures have yielded remains of Triassic lizards and early mammals.

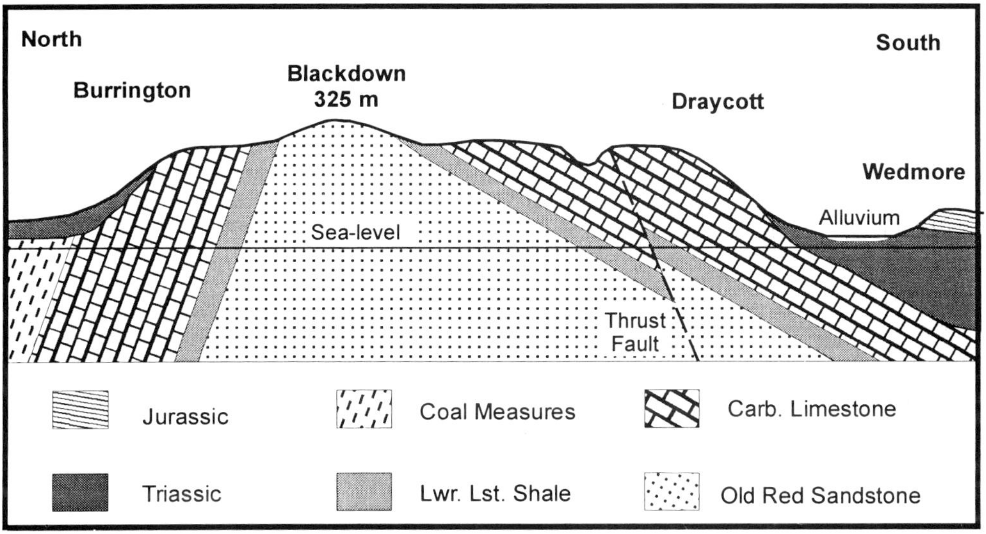

Schematic geological cross-section through the Mendips from Wedmore to Burrington.

About 200 million years ago at the close of the Triassic, the Rhaetic sea transgressed over the area, at times submerging almost the entire territory, leaving only a few emergent areas and creating the 'Mendip archipelago'. In this series of shallow lagoons the limestones and beach deposits of the Lower Jurassic were deposited. Silicification of these sediments has produced the cherts of the Harptree Beds. At times, tectonic activity caused reactivation and movement along some of the fault lines, producing local tension and the opening of fissures and joints. Subsequently infilled with Triassic and Jurassic material, these fissures, known as 'Neptunian Dykes', often extend tens or even hundreds of metres below the surface while remaining only a few metres wide. They provide evidence for essentially continuous sedimentation throughout the early Mesozoic. A good example of such a dyke can be seen in Gough's Cave, Cheddar, infilled with red Triassic material. Lead and zinc mineralisation also occurred at about this time, producing the orefields at Charterhouse, Shipham, Chewton Mendip and Priddy.

Eventually the sea level rose to submerge the entire area, producing spectacular horizontal marine wave-cut platforms such as that seen at Vallis Vale in eastern Mendip, upon which the hundreds of metres of Middle and Upper Jurassic and Cretaceous sediments were deposited. Even though buried, the Mendip 'axis' still continued to affect deposition and often produced much thinner sedimentary sequences than the neighbouring areas to the north and south. This sedimentation continued through until the Tertiary, about 20 million years ago. Only in the last few million years, following extensive erosion have the Mendip Hills re-emerged from their deep burial to give the present 'exhumed' topography we see today.

Geomorphology of the Mendip Hills

The geomorphology of the Mendip Hills reflects the complex geology and the long time span over which fluvial and periglacial erosion has acted. Much of the Mendip scenery can be explained by the removal of the impermeable cover rocks to reveal the old Triassic landscape beneath. As the Jurassic cover was eroded away, so the Carboniferous Limestone became exposed and cave development could begin. This occurred first in the west, and it is here that the oldest caves are found. Abandonment by their formative streams coupled with continued erosion has destroyed or blocked many of these caves and only a few truncated phreatic relicts are left. In central Mendip, the caves, although younger, are still actively forming, consequently this is where the largest and most complex caves are found. To the east, where the limestone has been exposed for a relatively short time, the caves are only just beginning to form and thus tend to be smaller and more immature (Fig. 4). An exception is the Stoke St Michael area where the limestone was exposed early by incision along the Mells river valley.

Similarly, the topography shows a progression from being most dissected in the west, to much more subdued relief in the east; where the hills hardly form a feature in the landscape rising only a little above the surrounding country. Again, this reflects the length of time erosion has had to act on the landscape. In the west, the limestone forms two ridges either side of the Lox Yeo valley, whereas in central and eastern Mendip the Old Red Sandstone forms prominent hills rising up to 100 m above the limestone plateau. This difference can be explained by the differing climate when the topography was produced. In western Mendip, much of the Old Red Sandstone was eroded during the Triassic which was dominated by a hot arid climate. Under these conditions, the sandstone is more susceptible to salt weathering and wind erosion than the limestone. In central and eastern Mendip most of the relief has formed over the last few million years, during which time erosion was dominated by a humid climate with more rapid dissolution of the limestone. Perhaps the most prominent feature is the Mendip plateau, an erosion surface at around 250 m O.D., resulting from subaerial planation during the Pliocene. The plateau is cut by a series of spectacular dry valleys and gorges. These gorges, such as at Cheddar, are not a product of collapsed caverns, but were formed by subaerial rivers during glacial periods. During these cold periods, when underground drainage was inhibited by permafrost, melt water runoff from snowcaps enabled surface rivers to carve out the gorges. During subsequent warm periods (such as the present interglacial) drainage returned underground and a new tier of caves was formed. This cycle has been repeated many times over the last million years. Today, drainage across the limestone is entirely underground except in some valleys in east Mendip and also during severe floods such as that of July 10th, 1968.

The surface of the plateau is pockmarked by numerous closed depressions. Most of these are developed in the Jurassic rocks and in valley fills. These 'suffusion dolines'

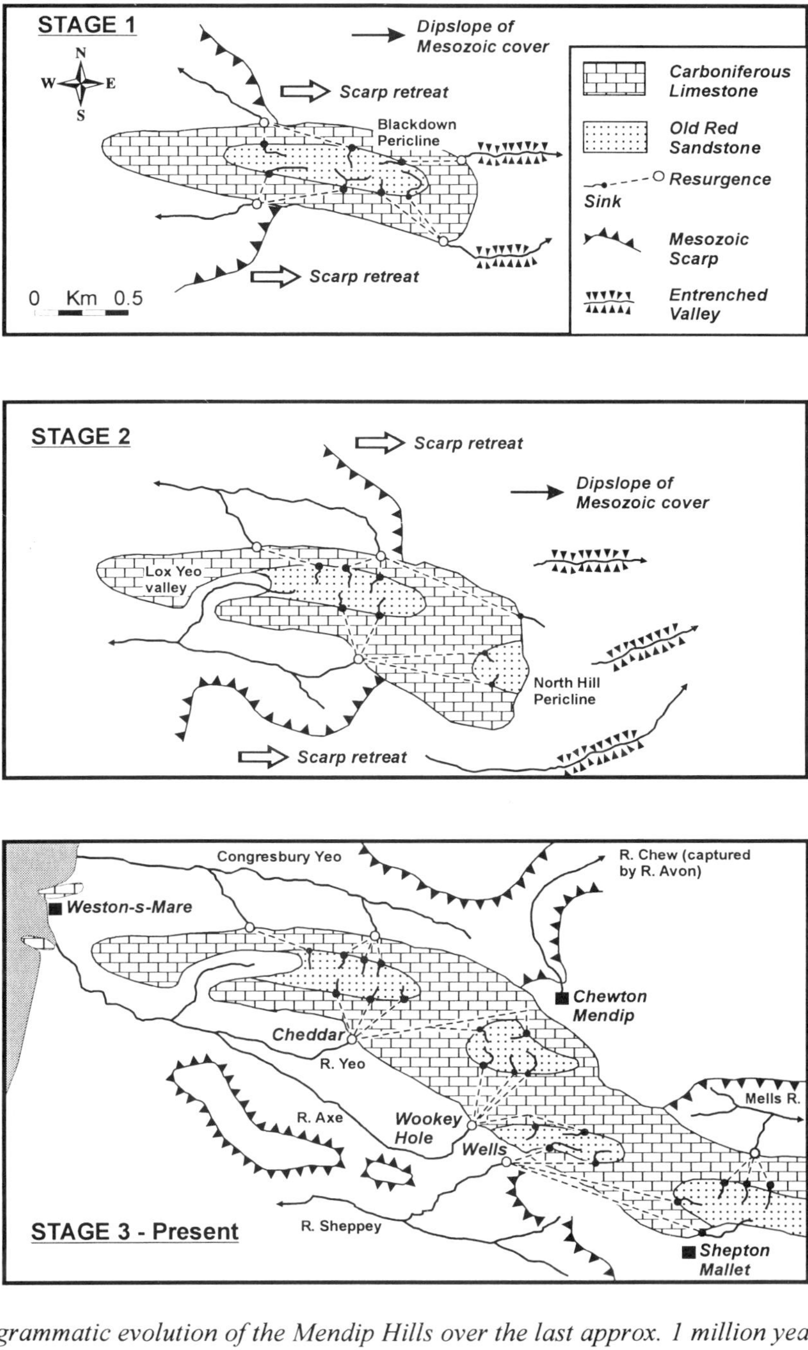

Diagrammatic evolution of the Mendip Hills over the last approx. 1 million years following the erosion of the younger cover rocks.

form where solution of the limestone has caused the subsidence of the thin overlying cover deposits; thus most of them are found along the feather-edge of the Jurassic Harptree Beds. Along the southern edge of the plateau lie a series of much larger closed depressions, such as that at Cross Swallet (NGR 516500). These were the site of small lakes during the glacial periods and are now partially infilled with lake deposits.

Geomorphology of the caves

The moderate to steep dips of the limestone in the Mendip Hills have produced a markedly different style of cave to that seen in other karst regions in Britain, unlike the long gently inclined passages seen in South Wales or the vadose shaft systems common in Yorkshire. A typical Mendip swallet cave is developed at the contact between the Lower Limestone Shales and the Carboniferous Limestone where the water flows off the impermeable shales into the limestone. The cave's upper passages are in the "vadose" zone, i.e. above the water-table. In this section the stream has a free air surface, flows on the floor of the passage cutting a narrow canyon and descends steeply, often down dip or along joints, via a series of small cascades or pitches. On reaching the water-table the passage enters the phreatic zone below the water-table (marked by a sump). Phreatic passages are water filled and thus dissolution takes place all around the conduit to produce rounded or elliptical passages. On Mendip with its moderate to steep dips these phreatic passages display a characteristic looping profile as the water flows down a bedding plane and then ascends up a joint or other fracture to gain higher bedding planes within the limestone en-route to the resurgence. In addition, the orientation of the cave, whether along strike or down dip, will have a marked effect on passage style; dip orientated passages will display a looping profile, strike sections will generally be shallower, sub-horizontal, passages.

Above the active streamway may lie a whole series of abandoned former stream courses now dry, either vadose or phreatic, or a combination of both, forming characteristic 'keyhole' shaped passages. Former directions of water flow can be ascertained from scallops on the passage walls. These shallow asymmetric scoop shaped hollows have their steeper side facing downstream. Furthermore, their size is related to the flow velocity. A rough rule of thumb is to divide 3.5 by the length (in centimetres) of a selection of scallops to give flow velocity in metres per second. These abandoned passages may become modified by breakdown and collapse, sediment or stalagmite deposition, or become reactivated or even destroyed at a later date.

Stalagmites and stalactites form when rainwater falling directly on to the limestone percolates down through the rock, gradually becoming saturated with calcium carbonate as it dissolves the limestone through which it passes. On reaching an open (vadose or abandoned) cave below, the calcium carbonate precipitates out to form stalactites and stalagmites. By measuring the ratio of uranium and thorium isotopes within these formations their absolute deposition dates, extending back to a maximum of half a million years, can be obtained. Other cave sediments can be dated using palaeomagnetic methods; by measuring the orientation of tiny magnetic clay particles within cave muds and comparing them to other deposits of known age (such as sea-floor basalts dated using other means), a comparative age can be obtained. Thus cave deposits can be important in their own right as they often preserve records of climate and drainage events during the cave's lifetime which can be dated. Moreover, much of this information is no longer preserved on the surface where erosion effectively wipes the slate clean; caves can thus be thought of as geological 'time-capsules'.

Floodwater in Cheddar Gorge, two days after the storm, July 1968.
Photo: courtesy of Pat Farrant

Today, the landscape is still in a state of flux. For the most part erosion occurs at rates unobservable to the human eye. However, major floods such as that of July 10th 1968 can cause seemingly profound changes in a short period of time. On that night, between ten and fifteen cm of rain fell over a wide area of the Mendips, causing severe flooding. Its causes and effects are documented by Hanwell and Newson (1970).

EXCURSION 1
CHEDDAR GORGE

DISTANCE: 6 km. Total height gain: 320 m.
PARKING: Ample parking is available in the many car parks at the lower end of the gorge. Alternatively, limited parking is available at Blackrock Gate. Cheddar is well served by bus routes from Wells, Weston-super-Mare and Bristol. In summertime, the gorge can become very busy with tourists.

Cheddar Gorge is one of Britain's best known karst features and attracts many thousands of visitors a year. However, the majority of these visitors do not visit the gorge's upper

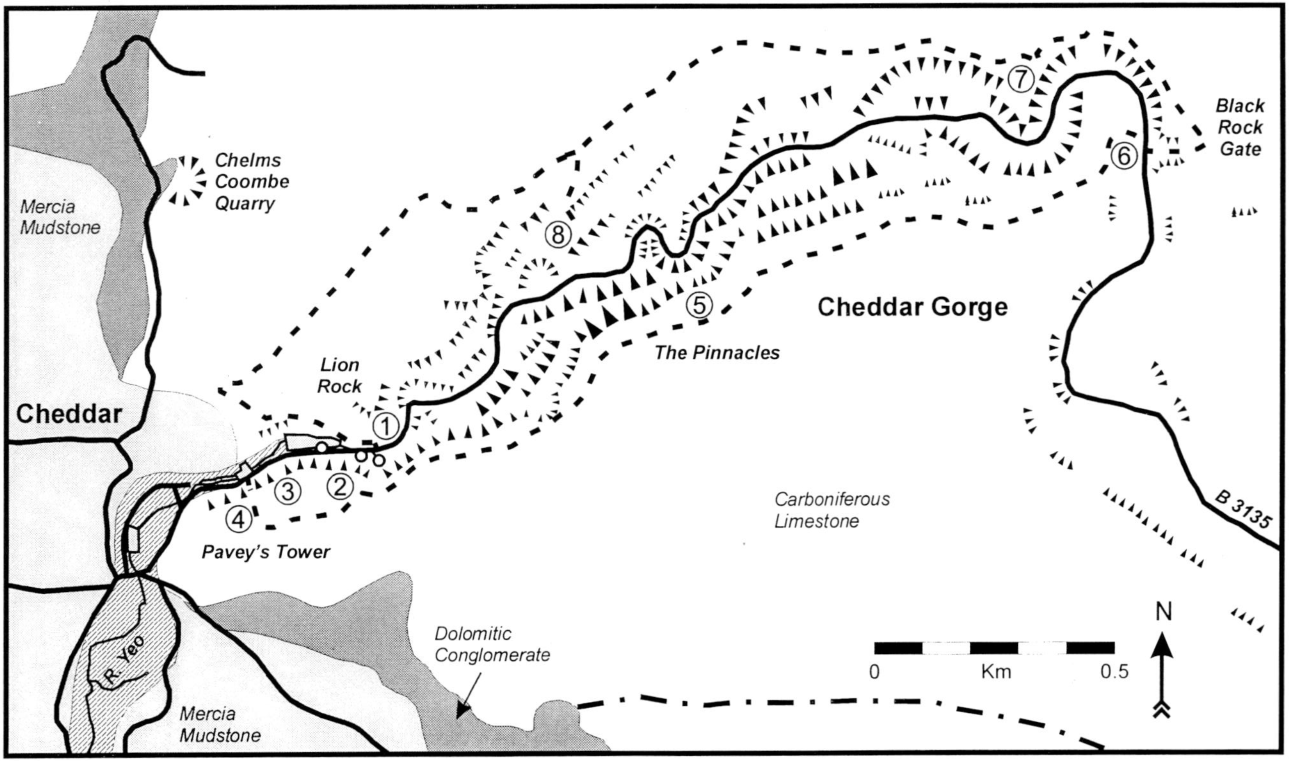

Cheddar Gorge (Excursion 1).

reaches, preferring to stay in the confines of the gift shops clustered in the village. The gorge itself provides a fine and easily accessible example of a karst gorge, with the added bonus of two show caves, which admirably display many of the attributes of a typical Mendip resurgence cave since abandoned by its formative river. The gorge, incised up to 120 m deep into the Clifton Down and Hotwells Limestones, descends from Cheddar Head (215 m) to the village of Cheddar (20 m) over a distance of two kilometres.

At the foot of the gorge lies the largest resurgence on Mendip. Above this lie several stacked tiers of caves, including both the show caves. These mark former outlets for the River Yeo, now abandoned following downcutting of the gorge and the development of new lower conduits. Although now dry, the gorge was incised over the last million years by successive phases of melt water erosion during cold climatic periods when underground drainage was restricted. Warmer periods, as at the present, allowed renewed cave development to take place forming new tiers of caves graded to the valley floor. This cycle has repeated itself many times over the last million years to produce the different cave levels seen today. Only during severe floods such as those of July 1968 does water still flow down the gorge. Above the gorge, the valley continues and splits to form part of a dendritic network of dry valleys extending over much of central Mendip. The excursion follows the circular gorge walk which is well marked.

1. Gough's Cave (ST 467639)

This is the larger of the two show caves in Cheddar and provides an admirable and easily accessible example of a phreatic cave. The ancestral River Yeo once flowed through the cave, but has now found a lower route following incision of the gorge. It now rises lower down the road, at point 2. Much of the initial section of the cave was sediment filled, but was excavated by R. C. Gough, who discovered the main cave in 1898. From the turnstiles, the cave descends past the Skeleton Pit where the remains of the 9000 year old Cheddar Man were excavated. DNA extracted from the teeth of this skeleton has been shown to match that of a local school teacher, a descendant by the female line. The water seen in the pit connects with the river outside and has been dived to a depth in excess of 20 m before the pit becomes too narrow. During floods, water rises here and fills the cave and occasionally water pours out through the turnstiles and down the road.

From Skeleton Pit the passage descends as a fine phreatic tube with an impressive series of joint aligned avens ascending into the roof. Close to the lowest point, the Fonts rise steeply to the right. These are a series of gour pools formed by stalagmite deposition. At this point the low roof has been blasted to form a easier route. Shortly beyond, the roof rises and is covered in at least two generations of large rounded phreatic scallops (asymmetric solutional hollows) giving the effect of beaten copper. Halfway up the slope a passage to the left leads to the 15 m deep shaft which was the first route to the present underground River Yeo to be discovered by divers, in 1985.

Further on up the steps, past some formations, the show cave passes through a blasted section, cutting through a 'Neptunian Dyke', a rift within the limestone infilled with much younger red Triassic marl. Immediately beyond lie the St Paul's and Diamond Chambers. Both have excellent examples of stalagmite formations. Behind St Paul's Chamber and only accessible to cavers, lies the main route to the underground river at Lloyd Hall.

Upstream from there, divers have penetrated through a sump into Bishops Palace, the largest chamber in the cave. The following two sumps are much deeper phreatic loops; the last, Sump Three, descends to a depth of 58 m, over 30 m below sea-level. The looping profile is characteristic of phreatic passages aligned down dip, unlike the show cave which is predominantly along strike and thus sub-horizontal. Diamond Chamber marks the furthest point in the show cave, although it is possible to enter a further series of phreatic passages and chambers on one of the 'Adventure Caving' trips. Dating of stalagmite within the cave demonstrates that the cave is about 250,000 years old.

A short distance up the gorge is the obvious roadside entrance to Cooper's Hole, an unsuccessful cavers' dig which is choked a short distance in. On the opposite side of the Gorge lie Pride Evans' Hole and Sun Hole, both short phreatic caves which have been excavated archaeologically.

2. Cheddar Risings and Saye's Hole (ST 466539)
Immediately below the entrance to Gough's Cave and adjacent to the tourist information centre lies the largest resurgence in the Mendips. The risings comprise two springs; the higher one is often dry in summer. Water also issues from about 16 points in the large pond downstream, which can be seen when the pond is drained. The combined mean flow is 18 million gallons per day. Proven feeders include most of the sinks along the southern flank of Blackdown and some further east including Tor Hole (ST 574520), about 11 km away. Behind the tourist information point lies the entrance to Saye's Hole. The large accessible entrance chamber rapidly narrows to a gated tube that enters a chamber with a lake. This has been dived but is soon choked, the water flowing to the resurgence immediately outside.

3. Cox's Cave (ST 464539)
Discovered by George Cox in 1837 following widening of the road, this is the shorter of the two show caves. It represents another short segment of abandoned phreatic conduit and was probably linked to Gough's Cave before valley incision truncated the two systems. It contains profuse stalagmite formations and displays some nice phreatic rifts and scalloping. The further reaches have been enlarged and modified in attempts to create a show cave to rival Gough's.

4. Pavey's Tower (ST 464538) and **Pulpit Rock** (ST 466538)
The tower, at the top of Jacob's Ladder (also reached by footpath from the other side of the hill), provides a fine viewpoint over the Somerset Levels and western Mendip. Two major quarries can also be seen; the larger is Batts Coombe quarry. If quarrying continues unchecked, the landscape which has taken millions of years to form could be leveled in only a few hundred.

Continuing up the hill, this small rock pulpit provides the first of many excellent platforms from which to view the gorge. The effect of the limestone dip on the appearance of the gorge is readily apparent; the northern side is far less precipitous because the southerly dip facilitates bedding plane slip. In contrast, the bold upstanding southern side

Cheddar Risings in 1928.
Photo: J.H. Savory, © University of Bristol Spelaeological Society

is relatively stable because the dip is into the cliffs. It has been remarked that 'while the southern side is bold, upstanding and conservative, the northern side may be considered as exceedingly liberal'. Strong north-south joints also considerably affect the cliff morphology in the gorge.

The meandering form and characteristic asymmetric 'V' shape is typical of fluvial excavation. The disparity in size between it and even the largest of Mendip caves, the lack of debris and the difference in longitudinal profile to that of the caves all contradict the notion that the gorge is a collapsed cavern. There can be no doubt that it resulted from river erosion during cold climatic periods. Even now, major floods such as that of July 1968 have the power to erode 6 m deep holes in the road. The dating of stalagmite from caves in the side of the gorge has enabled estimates of the rate of incision to be calculated; downcutting is proceeding at an average rate of 0.25 m per thousand years.

5. The Pinnacles (ST 473543)
This is one of the highest points in the gorge, from which it is possible to see the road 120 m below (*take care, the grass can be deceptively slippery*). From here, it is clearly apparent how the gorge has been incised into the Mendip Plateau. The sandstone ridge of Blackdown can be seen in the distance (see Excursion 2).

6. Blackrock Gate (ST 482545)
This is the confluence of two valley systems, one draining the Charterhouse area and the other draining from Priddy and the rest of central Mendip. A walk up the valley towards Charterhouse will provide a link with Excursion 2. From here, a walk down the other side of the gorge, passing points 7 and 8, will bring the walker back to Cheddar.

7. Bone Hole (ST 480547)
Tucked away in the undergrowth to the south of the path, immediately after the steep ascent from Blackrock Gate on the north side of the Gorge, is the large precipitous entrance to Bone Hole. Only the entrance area is accessible to non-cavers. Much of the stalagmite in the entrance area was removed as souvenirs to sell to the tourists in the 19th century. Beyond the entrance chamber, much of this cave was excavated by cavers and comprises a series of rifts aligned along major north-south joints. During the excavations, the cave diggers discovered large numbers of bones and artifacts dating from Beaker to Iron Age times. On cold frosty days, warm air rising out of cave can produce plumes of steam, a possible indication of an extensive cave system below, as yet un-entered. From here there is a fine view down the gorge.

8. Viewpoint (ST 470543)
This viewpoint, sign posted off the National Trust's 'Gorge Walk' along the north side of the gorge provides one of the best views of the gorge. From here, the prominent cliff opposite the viewpoint is High Rock, the highest sheer cliff in the gorge. Again, the role of the southerly dip and the jointing on the morphology of the gorge is clearly apparent. To the south the flat alluvial plains of the Somerset Levels can be seen.

EXCURSION 2

CHARTERHOUSE & BLACKDOWN

DISTANCE: 9 km. Total height gain: 150 m.
PARKING: Ample parking is available at the car park close to the crossroads at ST 505557.

Along the southern margin of Blackdown lies the hamlet of Charterhouse. Although by no means as well known as Cheddar or Burrington, this area contains many interesting features of a typical Mendip karst landscape. Here, several streams descend off the Old Red Sandstone slopes of Blackdown to sink along the contact between the Lower Limestone Shale and the Black Rock Limestone. Most of the stream sinks have been excavated by cavers, allowing access to several extensive swallet cave systems. Beyond the stream sinks the now dry valleys continue across the limestone outcrop, eventually to merge and descend into Cheddar Gorge, described in Excursion 1.

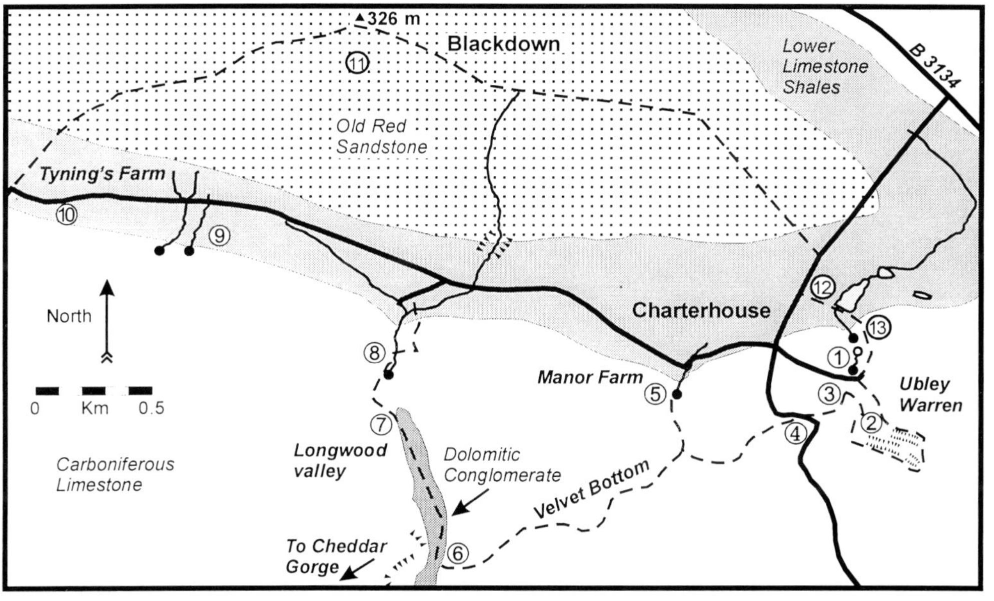

Charterhouse and Blackdown (Excursion 2).

Much of the area around Charterhouse has been affected by lead mining, initially in Roman times, but particularly during the 17th and 18th centuries. This has considerably modified the landscape, especially in Velvet Bottom, where the original valley form has been almost obliterated. In addition, the floods of July 1968 had a profound impact on the caves in the area. Not only was there severe flooding, both on the surface and underground, but the flood also caused many of the previously choked cave entrances to collapse, allowing access to cavers. Many of the Charterhouse caves were discovered in this way. In GB Cave, a surface collapse caused a glutinous mud flow to enter the cave altering overnight not only the cave but also many cherished views on how cave sediments are deposited. If so desired, this excursion can be linked with either the Cheddar Gorge excursion (Excursion 1) at Blackrock Gate (ST 482545), to form a long figure of eight loop, or to the Burrington excursion (Excursion 3) at the summit of Blackdown.

1. Blackmoor Swallet (ST 505555)
In the valley immediately adjacent to the car park is the sink for the Blackmoor stream. The stream sinks into an artificial conduit under a pile of mining debris; the original pre-mining stream sink cannot be seen. From here, dye tracing has shown the water takes three to four days to flow to the Cheddar Risings (Excursion 1, Point 2), over 200 m lower and four km distant. The excavation adjacent to the car park is an attempt to create a second entrance to Upper Flood Swallet, described at Point 13 at the end of the walk.

2. Ubley Warren Rakes (ST 508554)
This area south-east of the main valley is criss-crossed by a series of mineral rakes which have been extensively mined, starting in Roman times but mainly during the 17th and 18th centuries. Several capped shafts exist in the hummocky (known locally as 'gruffy') ground, mostly deriving from abortive attempts by Cornish miners to find lead ore at depth in the mid 1800's. Some of the rakes display good solutional features etched into the limestone.

Worked out mineral rake at Ubley Warren.
The dip of the limestone can be clearly seen.
Photo: A.R. Farrant

The prominent hillock with a mesh fence on the south side of Velvet Bottom marks the entrance to Stainsby's shaft, sunk by Cornish miners in the 1840's to a depth of 108 m in an abortive attempt to find lead ore. Most of the lead ore on Mendip lay close to the surface. The veins, unlike those in Derbyshire and Yorkshire, usually pinched out at depth. The shaft has since been re-excavated to a depth of 10 m by cavers.

3. Waterwheel Swallet and **Roman mines** (ST 505556)
Across the road from the stream sink, the gated cave entrance in the depression adjacent to the path is Waterwheel Swallet, dug into by cavers following a collapse during the 1968 floods. It is named after the remains of a six metre diameter waterwheel which was found in the entrance depression. The water was channeled here via a leat whose remains can still be seen to the north. After the abandonment of the waterwheel, the cave was used to wash away mine waste, much of which was found when the cave was first entered. The cave, a fossil stream sink for the Blackmoor stream, extends for 350 m and ends in a choked sump.

The hillside above the cave entrance, extending north-west towards the crossroads has been excavated by archaeologists who found direct evidence of Roman lead mining, including Roman coins and other artifacts. The Romans were mining galena (PbS, lead sulphide) along the veins or 'rakes'; these can be seen as narrow grooves running north-west up the hill. Very little other evidence of the Roman mines is left, most having been obliterated by later mining. Across the road to the north was the site of a small Roman fort. In the valley floor is the gated entrance to a disused 18th century lead mine, Grebe Swallet, whose entrance was washed open during the 1968 floods. The small alcove immediately below the track is a trial pit along the line of a thick calcite vein.

4. Velvet Bottom (ST 504555)
Just before the road embankment, some excellent 'buddle' pits can be seen in the valley floor. These circular walled pits were used to wash the lead ore using water piped from further up the valley. The rather incongruous pipe under the road was installed after the road embankment was washed away during the 1968 floods.

Between here and the confluence with the Longwood Valley, the valley has been much altered by mining activities. Much of the slag produced from the first phase of mining still contained a high proportion of lead. This was reworked and smelted in the 1800's and the resulting black glassy slag can be seen just downvalley from the Outdoor Pursuits Hut at the confluence with the Manor Farm tributary. Although poisonous to most plants, these slag heaps are important sites for several types of rare lichen which are tolerant of heavy metal concentrations.

5. Manor Farm Swallet (ST 498556)
A short distance up the tributary valley is Manor Farm Swallet. This cave, over a kilometre long and 154 m deep was discovered, after extensive digging, in 1973. Adjacent to the current blasted entrance shaft, the 1968 floods opened up a shaft 6.5 m by 8.5 m and 12 m deep. The cave, accessible only to experienced cavers, follows the typical Mendip swallet cave pattern with a series of small vadose inlet passages descending steeply down dip to

unite in a streamway before entering a large fossil phreatic passage. The cave terminates at an extensive boulder ruckle.

6. Timber Hole (ST 488548)

On the south side of the valley lies Timber Hole. This small shaft took some water during the 1968 floods. It has been dug by various groups over the years without success and is a good example of an influent vadose shaft, probably developed by a small intermittent melt water stream under cold climatic conditions. A little way on turn right at the junction, heading up the valley. Downvalley brings you out at Black Rock Gate (Excursion 1, point 6).

7. Longwood Valley Sink and **Rhino Rift** (ST 486555)

Walking up Longwood valley, a prominent dry stream trench becomes visible which carries a stream under major flood conditions. On the left-hand side, a shaft can be seen which marks the entrance to the Longwood Valley sink. This is a flood sink which was partially excavated by cavers in the hope of intersecting the stream beyond the present end of Longwood Swallet, but without success. A short distance upstream and up a tributary valley to the west lies the gated entrance to Rhino Rift. This vertical cave is a classic 'vadose invasion' shaft system, probably formed by a small melt water stream. It descends steeply via a series of five deep vadose shafts to a depth of 145 m. Dating of flowstone in the cave indicates it must be at least 75,000 years old.

"The Bridge", an isolated section of false floor in the Gorge, G.B. Cave.
Photo: S.B. Cottle

8. Longwood Swallet (ST 486557)
The major stream sink on the right hand side of the valley is Longwood Swallet. The concrete blockhouse entrance to the cave lies a short distance upstream. In flood the water flows past the sink and carries on down the valley to the Longwood Valley sink and in extreme floods, such as in 1968, all the way down Cheddar Gorge. The cave, the deepest known on Mendip at 175 m, contains over 1600 m of passage. It is entered by a natural shaft which penetrates a complex series of vadose streamways, rifts and chambers, These unite to join the Main Streamway, a vadose canyon which can be followed for over 500 m to a sump only 20 m above the resurgence level in Cheddar. Dye tracing and pulse wave tests have shown that at low flow, only 9% of the Longwood-Cheddar conduit is vadose, and that several discrete alternative conduits probably exist.

9. GB Cave and **Charterhouse Cave** (ST 476562)
This field (approach from the road) is owned by the Somerset Wildlife Trust. It contains the entrances to several caves and two stream sinks as it lies on the boundary between the Lower Limestone Shales and the Black Rock Limestone. The most significant is GB Cave, one of the best known and certainly the most studied cave on Mendip. The entrance is located under a blockhouse in a doline on the western side of the field. The cave is almost two km long and descends to a depth of 135 m. It follows the typical Mendip pattern of several vadose inlets amalgamating to form a large stream passage. The passage known as the "Gorge" and the "Main Chamber" is the largest in any Mendip cave, forming an impressive vadose canyon up to 10 m high and wide. The stream disappears into a massive boulder choke but a high level fossil phreatic passage can be followed into further chambers and passages. Comprehensive dating of the stalagmite formations has provided a wealth of information about the climatic oscillations during the Pleistocene, the development of the caves and the geomorphic history of the Mendip Hills.

To the east of the cave entrance lies the main stream sink, which can dry up during the summer months. The large fenced depression on the hilltop just to the south of the stream sink marks the site of a major collapse, caused by the 1968 floods, into GB Cave directly below. It caused a large glutinous mud flow into the cave, upon which pale bracken grew for up to a year afterwards.

A further 150 m to the east lies another stream sink at Read's Grotto. The cave into which the stream flows is only about 40 m long, but a short way above the sink lies the gated entrance to the 430 m long Charterhouse Cave. The stream enters this cave which is similar to, but unconnected with, the neighbouring GB Cave. Mining for lead ore has produced the gruffy ground to the south, which also contains some mineshafts. Tyning's Great Swallet lies 150 m to the south-east. This large depression appears to be a former stream sink, and is located directly over the lowest point in Charterhouse Swallet, about 60 m below. Two dug cave entrances can be seen; the one to the west ends in an unstable boulder collapse directly below the depression.

Calcite Formations in Bat Passage, an abandoned phreatic passage, G.B. Cave.
Photo: S.B. Cottle

10. Tyning's Barrows Swallet (ST 471563)
A shallow depression in the field south of the road contains the gated entrance to Tyning's Barrows Swallet, discovered in 1968 when flood water opened up the entrance shaft. Again, a series of vadose inlets merge to form a single streamway, ending at a choke almost beneath the tumuli in the south-west corner of the field. The stream has not been traced but it is thought to drain to Cheddar.

11. Blackdown and the **Mendip Plateau** (ST 484573)
Turning right at Tyning's Farm brings you up onto Blackdown. Old Red Sandstone forms the core of the Blackdown pericline and much sandstone can be seen on the tracks across Blackdown. The differing rock type produces a marked change in soil and vegetation type from that seen on the Carboniferous limestone and gives rise to boggy ground and surface drainage. From the summit of Blackdown (325 m) an excellent view of the Mendips can be gained on a clear day. To the south-east, the distant Old Red Sandstone summits of North Hill and Pen Hill (with the single mast) project above the flat limestone plateau. To the south, Cheddar Gorge is visible, beyond lie the Somerset Levels and the Quantock Hills. To the north lies Burrington Combe (described in Excursion 3).

12. Blackmoor (ST 506555)
In the field between the path and Charterhouse Outdoor Education Centre lies the site of a Roman Fort, presumably built to maintain and control the Roman mine working operations. The path crosses an embankment, behind which is a large lake which was dammed by the 18th century miners to provide water for washing the ore and to feed the leat which drained into Waterwheel Swallet. A little way upstream from here lies a series of partially infilled ponds and leats and the partly restored remains of the flues from the 18th century smelting works.

13. Upper Flood Swallet (ST 506558)
The gated entrance to this short, but pretty cave lies in the gruffy ground to the north of the car park. It is developed mainly in the Lower Limestone Shales and contains a small stream that flows to the Cheddar Risings.

EXCURSION 3

BURRINGTON COMBE

DISTANCE: 11 km. Total height gain: 300 m.
PARKING; Ample parking is available in the car parks at the bottom of Burrington Combe. Refreshments are available at the foot of the Combe and in Rickford. Burrington Turn is served by bus from Bristol.

Burrington Combe, cut into the northern flank of the Mendips provides a smaller but less commercialised example of a dry limestone gorge to that at Cheddar. It also provides a magnificent section through the Carboniferous Limestone and demonstrates the role of geology in determining the location and style of karst features. The Combe descends from about 200 m at Lower Ellick Farm down to the Mercia Mudstone lowlands to the north at around 80 m. The upper reaches of the Combe are strike orientated, after which it turns a sharp corner and cuts through the rest of the limestone succession at right angles to the strike. A well-developed alluvial fan is developed at the foot of the Combe. Two tributaries, the East and West Twin Brook valleys, descend steeply from the northern slopes of Blackdown, again providing good sections through the Carboniferous Limestone, the Lower Limestone Shales and the Old Red Sandstone. Like the gorges at Cheddar and Ebbor it was cut during cold climatic periods when permafrost prevented underground drainage. Most of the caves described are stream sinks along the limestone-shale contact, the water resurging along the northern flank of the Mendips. The steep dip, up to 70°, has influenced the cave morphology in the area. Many of the caves descend steeply down dip to the water table, and have become choked with washed in material. As a consequence, the water has often had to find alternative routes, facilitated by the numerous fractures, producing complex bouldery phreatic mazes.

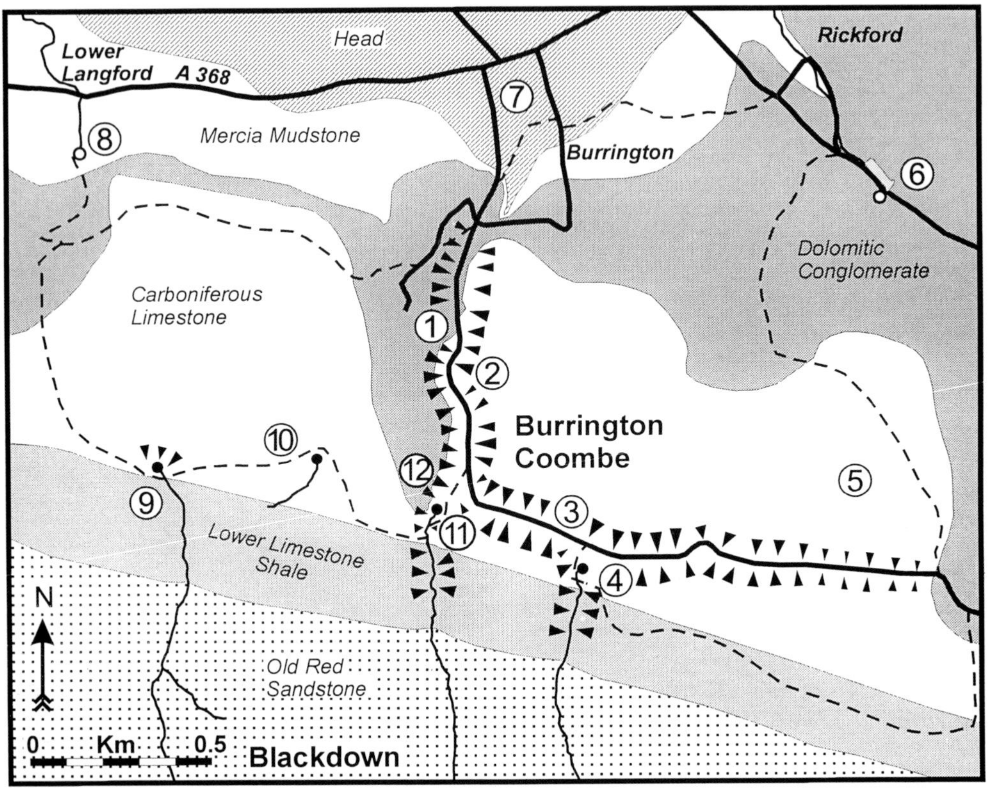

Burrington Combe and Blackdown (Excursion 3).

1. Rock of Ages (ST 476587) and **Plumley's Hole** (ST 476587)
The prominent crag of steeply dipping Burrington Oolite across the road from the toilet block at the base of Burrington Combe, is the Rock of Ages immortalised by the Rev. Toplady in his hymn of that title. The story runs that he was inspired to compose the hymn whilst sheltering in the crevice at the foot of the crag during a rainstorm.

Opposite the Rock of Ages, in an alcove at the base of the cliff is the site of Plumley's Hole. This cave, opened by quarrying, was said to be a natural shaft 45 m deep with a stream at the base; although these claims have yet to be substantiated. It was named after Joe Plumley, a local man, who was lowered down on a rope to investigate. While being hauled out, he became caught beneath a lip and his neck was broken. In the adjacent disused quarry, the prominent rib running diagonally down the cliff is a thin band of dolomite. Behind the toilet block lies a small patch of reddish Triassic Dolomitic Conglomerate. The next two points are adjacent to the road up the valley.

2. Aveline's Hole (ST 476587)
Having been discovered in 1797 by two men digging for rabbits, this gaping hole adjacent to the road was largely excavated by archaeologists, including William Boyd Dawkins,

who named the site after his friend, William Aveline. Several human skeletons and a rich Late Palaeolithic (about 10,000 years ago) fauna were found. The cave is a fine example of a phreatic tube, and probably once functioned as a resurgence. The main passage extends for a short distance to a muddy choke and can be explored with a good torch, appropriate footwear and care.

3. Lionel's Hole (ST 480582)
The entrance to this cave is a small hole, behind some bushes across the road from the confluence of the East Twin Brook valley with the Combe. The cave extends west along the strike as a close-knit three-dimensional collapse maze. The scree slopes along the north side of the combe, down valley from the entrance, are good places to collect fossils from the Black Rock Limestone.

4. East Twin Swallet (ST 480581)
A little way up the tributary valley, the East Twin stream disappears into this gaping hole developed close to the shale-limestone boundary, reappearing at both Rickford (after 6 hours) and Langford Risings (17 hours). The water cannot be followed far underground, but reappears in Pierre's Pot in the West Twin Brook valley (point 12). Above the streamway, suitably equipped cavers can follow a series of small passages for approximately 300 m. This part of the cave was originally entered via another entrance, Spar Pot, since infilled. If one continues up the steep East Twin valley, several other stream sinks can be found. Each one is developed in a thick limestone bed within the Lower Limestone Shales. Ultimately the valley will bring you out on to the Old Red Sandstone on Blackdown and can be linked to the walk at Charterhouse (Excursion 2) if so desired.

5. Burrington Ham (ST 488583)
On a clear day, pleasant views across to Wales and north to the limestone upland of Broadfield Down (ST 5065), which closely resembles the Mendips in its geology, geological history and structural setting, can be seen from here.

6. Rickford Rising (ST 487591) and **Rickford Combe** (ST 490590)
This spring, issuing from an impenetrable rift in the Dolomitic Conglomerate, together with that at Langford, are the risings for all the Burrington caves. Downstream, leads to the 'Plume of Feathers' which supplies liquid of a different sort.

Upstream from the spring this large sinuous dry valley continues for another kilometre, incised over 60 m into hard Dolomitic Conglomerate, but ends somewhat anomalously with its upper end 'hanging' above Blagdon Lake. Previously thought to be an overflow channel for an ice dammed lake, a more likely origin is that the Congresbury Yeo (not the same river Yeo as that at Cheddar) originally flowed through it. The river's course was superimposed onto the harder Dolomitic Conglomerate from the cover of softer Jurassic rocks, since eroded. Continued erosion of the softer rocks in the Vale of Wrington to the north has led to the abandonment of the valley by the Congresbury Yeo. A small intermittent spring by the road, Squire's Well, may be an overflow for Rickford Rising.

Steeply dipping limestone (Burrington Oolite) in the Rock of Ages, Burrington Combe.
Photo: A.R. Farrant

7. Burrington Turn (ST 477595)
The gentle slope, which the main road ascends to Burrington Turn, is a result of the large alluvial fan that has developed at the foot of the Combe. Melt water torrents during the cold glacial periods deposited their debris on the low ground at the mouth of the valley, gradually over time building up the alluvial fan. In severe storms such as that of 1968, much debris can still be washed down and deposited in the surrounding fields.

8. **Langford Risings** (ST 466593)
This large spring, dammed by Bristol Water PLC, together with its larger companion at Rickford, drains most of the Burrington area. Most of the swallet water probably combines into a single streamway before splitting again to flow to the two separate resurgences.

9. Read's Cavern (ST 468584)
Originally called Keltic Cavern after the Early Iron Age occupants who, it is believed, abandoned the site after a rock fall. This cave consists of a large chamber with several unstable routes below. As with all the stream sinks in Burrington, it lies at or close to the shale-limestone boundary, the water draining to Rickford and Langford.

10. Bos Swallet, Drunkards' Hole, Rod's Pot, and **Bath Swallet** (ST 472584)
Adjacent to the track lie a series of deep dolines, four of which contain small caves. All the penetrable caves descend steeply down dip, before ending in chokes. The first and highest is Bos Swallet. The entrance depression here was archaeologically excavated and many artifacts including Beaker age pottery and flint implements were found. The second is Drunkards' Hole, Rod's Pot is the next, one of the more popular novice caving trips on Mendip, and finally the active stream sink at Bath Swallet, so called after the stone bath, now destroyed, constructed by a caving club for their hut nearby. The water resurges at Rickford and Langford Risings.

11. West Twin Brook Adit (ST 475582) and **Goatchurch Cavern** (ST 476582)
The curious stone trough beside the path up the West Twin Brook is the outfall for the West Twin Brook Adit, the gated entrance of which can be found a short distance upstream. The adit was driven to tap the Old Red Sandstone aquifer. It cuts through the Lower Limestone Shales and the Old Red Sandstone, much of the debris being tipped down the valley. However, the water yield was much less than had been hoped and the scheme was a failure.

A short distance up the east bank from the trough lies Goatchurch Cavern, one of Mendip's most popular caves for novice cavers. Two entrances lead into a complex three-dimensional phreatic maze, descending steeply with the 60° dip to a depth of about 60 m. The first section of the upper entrance can be followed with a good torch and care. The floor (often slippery!) has steps cut into it and the remains of railings, dating from when the cave was briefly operated as a show cave around 1901. Large rounded scallops and the elliptical shape of the passage indicate its phreatic origin, flowing slightly aslant the strike of the rock. At the end a large stalagmite bank chokes the passage. Several steeply descending passages mark the continuation of the cave down dip. The cave is an abandoned former stream sink.

12. Sidcot Swallet (ST 475583), **Flange Swallet** (ST 475583) and **Pierre's Pot** (ST 476584)
Further downstream another former stream sink, Sidcot Swallet can be explored by cavers for around 250 m through a series of small passages. The hillside opposite is covered with tipped shale from the adit upstream. A short distance downvalley the stream sinks into Flange Swallet. This choked sink, once dug out to a depth of 10 m, takes most of the water flowing down the valley, resurging at Rickford and Langford risings. In wet conditions, the water continues past the swallet to sink further down the valley. Several other small phreatic caves can be found nearby. One of these, in trees adjacent to the track, is the rift entrance to Pierre's Pot. Interestingly, the streamway in the lower part of this cave is derived not from the close by Flange Swallet, but from the East Twin Brook valley. Thus the water drains along strike from East Twin Swallet into the Pierre's Pot streamway, before flowing stratigraphically up through the limestone to resurge at Rickford and Langford. From here a walk back down the Combe will bring the walker to the Rock of Ages.

EXCURSION 4

PRIDDY & NORTH HILL

DISTANCE: 11 km. Total height gain: 100 m.
PARKING: There is ample parking at Stock Hill Forest (ST 549513) and several good pubs in Priddy for refreshment. The Hunter's Lodge Inn is the main social meeting place for cavers on Mendip.

The Priddy area contains many superb karst features, including Mendip's longest and most complex caves. A multitude of small streams rise on the Old Red Sandstone slopes of North Hill, before sinking at the contact with the overlying Black Rock Limestone. Most of the water ascends stratigraphically through the limestone via a series of deep phreatic loops to resurge at Wookey Hole, but on the eastern margin of North Hill the story is more complicated. Here, Triassic Dolomitic Conglomerate overlies the Old Red Sandstone and Carboniferous Limestone. Some streams sink into the Conglomerate, eventually passing into the Carboniferous Limestone at depth, to resurge at Rodney Stoke Risings (ST 487503) or Wookey Hole (Excursion 5), demonstrating the heterogeneous nature of karstic aquifers. Furthermore, both the surface topography and the underground drainage have been much modified by the activities of lead miners. The pock marked ground bears testament to the enormous amount of mining activity that has taken place. Little can grow on the contaminated land except forestry and Stock Hill Forest now covers much of the main ore field. Unlike the underground drainage, the dry valleys incised into the plateau converge at the head of Cheddar Gorge, demonstrating that surface drainage patterns are here completely unrelated to underground ones.

1. Five Buddles Sink (ST 547514)
Adjacent to the road is a prominent stream sink by a gated shaft. This is Five Buddles sink. Across the road is an alternative shaft entrance. The sink is developed in Triassic Dolomitic Conglomerate. The shaft enters a short stretch of adit in which some old mining artifacts were found. It may be the site of Thomas Bushell's attempt to drive an adit to drain the local mines in the 17th century. The water resurges at Rodney Stoke and thus must either traverse the Old Red Sandstone via a fault or flow through the Dolomitic Conglomerate and into the Carboniferous Limestone at depth, either to the north or south of the sandstone pericline. In order to do this; the water must cross over known flow routes either from St Cuthbert's Swallet to Wookey or Tor Hole (ST 574520) to Cheddar. Between here and the next stop are many pits, ponds and spoil heaps, which are the legacy of former lead mining activities. Most of the mine workings lay to the east in what is now forestry land, the ore being brought to the main valley for washing and processing where water was available.

2. St Cuthbert's Leadworks (ST 545505)
A collection of ruined buildings is all that is left of the St. Cuthbert's Leadworks, which was operational until the early 1900's. Most of the visible ruins are a legacy from the 19th century re-smelting operations. The original mine waste from earlier mining still contained

a high proportion of lead and was re-smelted, the resultant characteristic black slag occurs in abundance around the site.

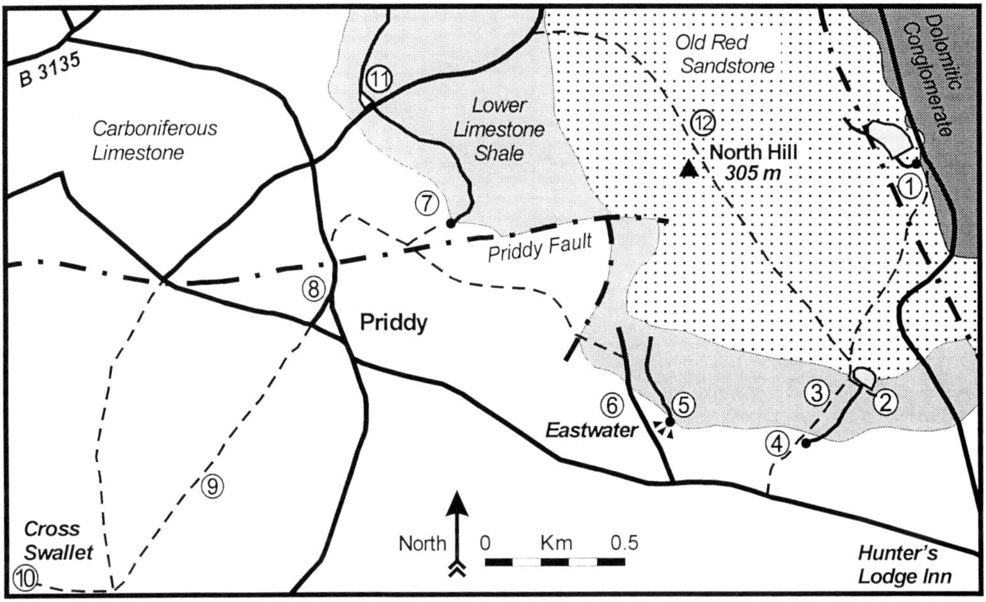

Priddy and North Hill (Excursion 4).

3. Plantation Swallet (ST 543506)

A shallow trench across the footpath is all that remains of the stream that used to sink in the now choked entrance to Plantation Swallet, a large mined passage dug by the lead smelters attempting to divert water from the mine workings in the valley. The water vanished into impenetrable fissures eventually to enter St. Cuthbert's Swallet 60 m lower.

4. St. Cuthbert's Swallet (ST 543505)

In the depression south of the path is St. Cuthbert's Swallet, the second longest cave on Mendip, at nearly 7 km, and certainly the most complex. It lies, as with most swallet caves, at the contact between the Lower Limestone Shales and the Black Rock Limestone and has developed along both sides of a plunging anticline which has been cut by several thrust faults. All that can be seen on the surface is the ubiquitous capped shaft adjacent to the main stream sink. The water entering the cave can be 'turned off' using a dam at the sink to allow cavers an easier ascent of the narrow entrance rift. Below the cave entrance, several vadose streamways enter a complex multi-level series of well decorated collapse chambers and passages before the streams amalgamate and flow into a long joint controlled rift to enter a sump 140 m lower. The water has been dye traced to Wookey

Hole in about eight hours, thus confirming an earlier trace made in 1860. This provided the basis for a successful lawsuit in 1863 by the owners of Wookey Hole Paper Mill against the St. Cuthbert's Leadworks for polluting the stream.

St. Cuthbert's Minery in the late 19th century.
Photo from the A.E. Mc R. Pearce collection

5 .Eastwater Cavern (ST 538506)

Eastwater Cavern provides a classic example of a stream sink and blind valley developed at the boundary between the Lower Limestone Shale and the Black Rock Limestone, a good exposure of which can be seen at the cave entrance. The entrance is a 25 m deep nightmare of loose unstable boulders. Below, the cave extends for over 2 km; much of which is a complex series of bedding plane passages, rifts and fault controlled shafts, including the 55 m deep Primrose Pot. The stream has been traced to Wookey Hole in about 16 hours.

6. North Hill Swallet (ST 535551)
The piped entrance shaft is all that is visible on the surface of this small cave, which extends for 260 m. Much of the passage was enlarged by blasting when the cave was being dug by cavers.

7. Swildon's Hole (ST 531513)
A rather incongruous stone blockhouse marks the entrance to Swildon's Hole, the longest and one of the most popular caves on Mendip. Once again, water draining the Old Red Sandstone of North Hill sinks in a blind valley on reaching the Black Rock Limestone. Experienced cavers can explore over 9 km of passage. From the entrance a fine vadose streamway descends steeply to the west, until it reaches Sump One, almost under Priddy church. From here the stream turns along the strike through eleven more sumps, passing under Priddy Green. The furthest point yet reached lies 170 m directly below the Queen Victoria pub, east of Priddy Green. Above the streamway lies a network of phreatic passages and vadose inlets, now abandoned by the stream, forming a complex series of interconnected passages. At least three main phases of cave development have been identified. The earliest passages may have originally drained to Cheddar. The present stream now flows to Wookey Hole in about 25 hours.

8. Priddy Green Sink (ST 527511)
Adjacent to the road outside Manor Farm is the inconspicuous entrance to Priddy Green Sink. Flooding of the road led cavers to excavate the sink; which eventually formed a tortuous link via several vertical pitches (the aptly named 'Cowsh Avens'), to the Swildon's Four streamway below.

9. Twin Titties Swallet (ST 522504)
South of Priddy Green and named after the two shapely depressions in which the cave is located is a long standing cave dig, which reached a depth of over 60 m, nearly all of which had to be excavated. It appears to be another example of a 'vadose invasion' cave similar to Rhino Rift (Excursion 2).

10. Cross Swallet (ST 515500)
Cross Swallet is the name given to a large cruciform closed basin, 500 m in diameter and over 10 m deep. It forms one of Mendip's best examples of a closed basin. Initially formed by solutional activity during warm phases of the Pleistocene, the sinks in the floor of the depression were blocked by permafrost during the ensuing cold spell. Melt water became ponded, eroding the prominent terrace, depositing the thick clays on the floor of the depression and occasionally spilling over to form the overflow channel to the south. More recent erosion has produced the 8 m deep sink in the centre of the basin, which drains the impermeable clay floor. Fissures here have been penetrated for about 10 m depth before becoming too tight. A short walk to the south provides an excellent view across the Somerset Levels and to Glastonbury Tor, the largest of many Jurassic outliers rising above the Levels. If so desired, this walk can be combined with that at Wookey Hole and Ebbor Gorge (Excursion 5), 2 km to the south-east.

11. Priddy Pool (ST 528517)
Priddy Pool forms the headwaters of the Swildon's Hole stream and should not be confused with the St. Cuthbert's Minery pool (ST 545508) which is also referred to, incorrectly, as Priddy Pool. Downstream lies a pumping station, obtaining water from a 33 m deep borehole in the Lower Limestone Shales. This is an important source for the Swildon's Hole stream, which is often reduced to a trickle during periods of abstraction.

12. North Hill (ST 540514)
North Hill is, at 307 m A.O.D., one of the highest points on Mendip. Here, like Blackdown and Pen Hill, the more resistant Old Red Sandstone exposed in the core of the North Hill pericline forms a prominent hill rising above the generally flat Mendip Plateau. Being impermeable, the sandstone supports surface drainage, feeding all the streams, which eventually sink into the caves when they reach the limestone. On a clear day, most of central Mendip can be seen from this point, with the long ridge of Blackdown visible to the north-west. From here a short walk brings you back to the car park.

This excursion can be shortened by 3 km if points 9 and 10 are omitted, but these two sites provide good examples of karst features away from the shale-limestone boundary.

EXCURSION 5
WOOKEY HOLE AND EBBOR GORGE

DISTANCE: 10 km. Total height gain: 350 m.
PARKING: There is ample parking at the Ebbor Gorge car park (ST 521484), which also has picnic facilities and a nature trail. Wookey Hole has the usual tourist facilities and a pub for refreshment. Like Cheddar, it can get crowded on busy summer weekends. Wookey is served by bus from Cheddar and Wells.

As with its more famous neighbour at Cheddar, the Wookey area contains both a show cave and a fine example of a limestone gorge. The area lies on the southern flank of the Mendips close to the city of Wells. Here, the Carboniferous Limestone is dipping to the south at 25-30° and is overlain by Millstone Grit and Lower Coal Measures. The geology is complicated by a series of thrust faults. Younger Triassic and Jurassic deposits lie unconformably over the limestone. Wookey Hole is the second largest resurgence on Mendip. However, there are marked differences between Wookey and Cheddar, not least the differing geology. At Ebbor, a thin slice of impermeable Millstone Grit and overlying Coal Measures forms a barrier to water flow within the limestone, which is absent at Cheddar. However, at Wookey Hole this barrier was breached by erosion during Triassic times. The resulting ravine subsequently became infilled with a poorly sorted mixture of limestone and sandstone fragments, since cemented together to form the Dolomitic Conglomerate, which, like the Carboniferous Limestone, is permeable. This permeability enabled water to drain out of the limestone once the overlying softer Jurassic rocks had been removed by erosion.

1. Ebbor Thrust Fault (ST 522484) and **Primrose valley** (ST 523484)
A prominent line of cliffs to the east of the steeply descending path from the Ebbor Gorge car park marks the lines of the Ebbor Thrust Fault. Here a slice of the Carboniferous Limestone (Burrington Oolite) has been thrust up over the younger quartzitic sandstones and shales of the Lower Coal Measures and Millstone Grit. The base of the cliffs marks the contact, although scree and weathering products bury the actual fault. The prominent Primrose valley into which the path descends has been excavated along the strike of the less resistant shales. Several small caves can be found along the base of the cliff but most are of archaeological interest only. In one, a Bronze Age gold bracelet was found during an archaeological dig in the 1950's.

The small stream flowing down the valley is a consequence of the impermeable Lower Coal Measures, which outcrop in the valley floor. Downstream, the water gradually sinks into the Dolomitic Conglomerate, which overlies the Coal Measures to the south-west.

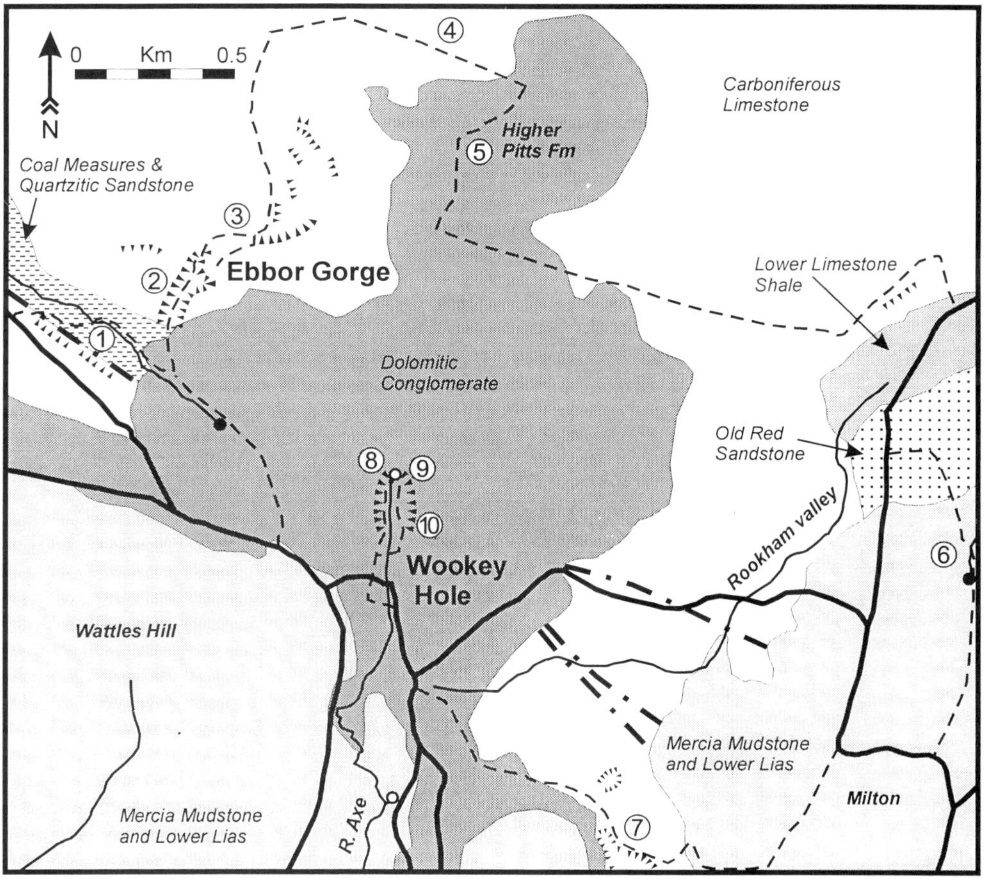

Wookey Hole and Ebbor Gorge (Excursion 5).

2. Ebbor Gorge (ST 525486)
Continuing on across the footbridge, a valley confluence is reached. Shortly after turning left up the tributary valley, the valley sides close in and become more vertical. The valley is now incised in the Carboniferous Limestone, lying stratigraphically below the Millstone Grit. The valley becomes increasingly gorge like with ivy mantled cliffs and scree slopes 25-50 m high. The screes are impressive reminders of the Pleistocene cold phases. At the narrowest point, aptly named 'The Narrows', the gorge is more reminiscent of an unroofed vadose cave passage. The steep section here forms a prominent 'knick point'. This marked change in valley gradient results from valley rejuvenation during the Pleistocene cold periods. Each successive phase of valley incision is graded to a new lower base level as a consequence of regional lowering to the south, producing a series of knick points, which gradually migrate up the valley as erosion proceeds.

At the top of The Narrows, a small stream rises only to sink after a short distance in the scree. Cave fragments line either side of the gorge and some may ultimately prove to be fossil resurgences of the adjacent Wookey Hole system. Several of these small caves have yielded Late Pleistocene faunas. Ebbor was formed in much the same way as Cheddar Gorge, by summer melt water runoff during cold phases in the Pleistocene, when underground drainage was prevented by permafrost. Today, the majority of the drainage is underground. The reason for the much smaller size of Ebbor compared to Cheddar is the difference in catchment area. Cheddar drained most of the Mendip Plateau while Ebbor's catchment is limited to a few square kilometres.

3. Upper Ebbor (ST 527493)
Above the highest knick point the valley opens out into a gently descending meandering dry valley draining part of the Mendip Plateau. A short detour along the path to the right leads to a fine viewpoint.

4. Sandpit Hole (ST 532498)
400 m north of Dursdon Drove, across farm land lies Sandpit Hole. This large, tree filled, pit some 13 m deep contains several small caves. It may represent a collapsed cavern. Excavations by cavers show that boulders continue to at least 16 m below the surface.

5. Higher Pitts Farm Iron Mine (ST 535492)
Haematite intermixed with earthy manganese ores was worked during the 1890's by the ill-fated Somersetshire Manganese and Iron Ore Company Ltd. in the vicinity of Higher Pitts Farm. The ore, worked from pods and veins in the Dolomitic Conglomerate, was associated with calcite, cerrusite (lead carbonate) and copper minerals, plus a unique assemblage of rare secondary lead, copper and manganese minerals. These minerals, Mendipite, Chloroxiphite and Diaboleite are rare or unknown outside the Mendip area. Little is left to see on the surface, most of the pits having being filled in and the spoil tips leveled. From here, a shortcut can be taken straight to Wookey Hole (point 8) if so desired. Good views of Wells, Glastonbury and the Somerset Levels can be seen from the path en-route to Rookham.

6. Welsh's Green Swallet (ST 550477)
This is a rather unusual cave, developed not in Carboniferous Limestone but where a stream draining an area of Jurassic Lower Lias clay sinks on reaching the underlying Blue Lias Limestone. However, the water must flow into and through the Carboniferous Limestone at depth in order to reach the resurgence at St Andrew's Well (ST 552459), in Wells. The cave has been excavated by cavers and currently exceeds 400 m in length.

7. Underwood Quarry (ST 539468)
In 1935, quarrying opened a series of fissures containing an Ipswichian interglacial fauna (dating back to about 120,000 years ago) including hippo and straight tusked elephant. The remains are in Wells Museum.

8. Wookey Hole (ST 532480)
Wookey Hole is one of three show caves on Mendip, the other two being at Cheddar (Excursion 1), and is the second largest resurgence. It provides an easily accessible example of a resurgence cave. The cave is unusual in that much of it is developed in Triassic Dolomitic Conglomerate. The horizontal bedding and prominent vertical jointing produce a markedly different style of cave to that formed in dipping Carboniferous Limestone. The subterranean Axe has been followed upstream by divers through a series of sumps to the current limit of exploration at Wookey 25. The river drains much of central Mendip, including most of the caves in the Priddy area.

Exposures of the Dolomitic Conglomerate are well exhibited in the entrance passage, an abandoned resurgence of the River Axe. Descending 'Hell's Ladder' enables the visitor to see the present underground River Axe. The 'Witch of Wookey' is a fine example of a stalagmite boss, although unfortunately previous visitors have removed many of the formations in the cave. Archaeologists found evidence of a Romano-British cemetery in Chamber Four. Beyond, the show cave (partly mined) enters a splendid series of rift chambers developed along prominent joints, to enter Chamber Nine. A leak in the floor of this chamber has been dye-traced to Glencott Spring, 1 km to the south. Given time, this will eventually capture all the water from Wookey. Chamber Nine is the limit for non-cavers, but a climb in the far corner enables experienced cavers to enter a well decorated high level passage, which can be followed almost to the surface. This passage acted as a former resurgence for the ancestral River Axe.

A short distance upstream the cave emerges from the Carboniferous Limestone, and the passage form changes to a series of deep phreatic loops. The deepest point yet reached in Wookey 25 is some 60 m below water level. The mined route out to the surface from the show cave section provides a good exposure of Dolomitic Conglomerate.

9. Wookey Resurgence (ST 532480)
On leaving the show cave, a detour to the left will provide a picturesque view of the Axe resurgence. A sluice controls the water level, with the leat feeding water to the paper mill down the valley.

10. Wookey Ravine (ST 532480) and **Hyaena Den** (ST 532479)
The deep rocky ravine immediately downstream of Wookey Hole is unlike many other gorges on Mendip in that there are no feeder valleys. Instead the ravine is probably a product of cliff retreat and cavern collapse, known as a 'steephead'.

When discovered by workmen digging the leat in 1852 the Hyaena Den was completely filled with sediment. Extensive archaeological excavations have yielded many Pleistocene remains. The site was used both by Palaeolithic Man and by hyaenas. On the hillside above are two other small caves dug open by archaeologists, Badger Hole and Rhinoceros Hole, which have also yielded many artifacts. Many of these can be seen in Wookey Hole Museum.

The circular walk can be completed by following the West Mendip Way up the lower Ebbor Gorge until one reaches point 1 (above).

EXCURSION 6

STOKE ST. MICHAEL AND BEACON HILL

DISTANCE: 10 km. Total height gain: 350 m.
PARKING: There is parking in Stoke St. Michael, which has a pub for refreshment.

Over much of eastern Mendip the geologically recent exhumation of the limestone from its cover of Jurassic and younger rocks, coupled with generally low relief, has precluded the development of large or vertically extensive caves like those seen elsewhere on Mendip. However, although not as well developed as the central Mendips, the eastern Mendips do have some interesting karst features. The best developed karst landscape occurs in the Stoke St. Michael area. Here, incision by the Mells River has provided the relief for cave development to occur and allowed for early removal of the Jurassic cover, while the impermeable ridge of Silurian andesitic lavas and Devonian Old Red Sandstone provides the catchment area for numerous small swallet streams. The limestone outcrop here is relatively narrow, often not much more than a kilometre wide. This is primarily a function of the steep dip, often up to 70°, which also has had a profound effect on the style of cave development. Nearly all the water sinking at the swallets on the north side of Beacon Hill resurges at two major groups of springs, St. Dunstan's Well and Ashwick Grove risings.

The relatively narrow outcrop of limestone is clearly identifiable by its flatness and towards the east, by the numerous quarries which are destroying in a handful of years what nature took hundreds of thousands, if not millions of years, to create. Towards Frome the limestone is covered by the Jurassic Inferior Oolite. The contact is marked by a spectacular flat unconformity, in essence a fossil sea-floor complete with encrusting oysters and infilled worm burrows, best seen at Vallis Vale (ST 756491) or Tedbury camp (ST 746489).

1. Moons Hill Quarry (ST 660450)

The large quarry upstream of Stoke St. Michael is excavated in Silurian andesitic lavas and ash deposits, the remains of an ancient volcano. At around 420 million years old these are the oldest rocks exposed on Mendip. Being impermeable, the ground and footpath are often wet and support surface drainage.

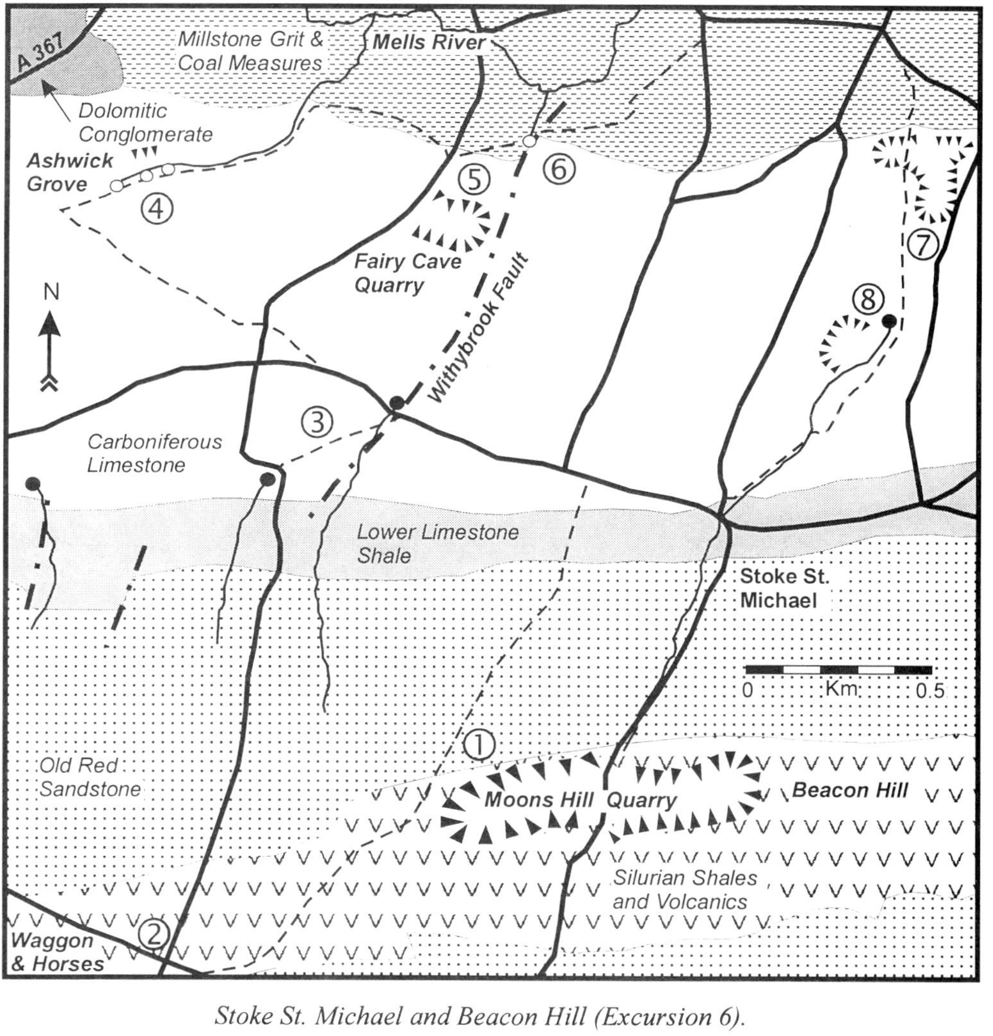

Stoke St. Michael and Beacon Hill (Excursion 6).

A phreatic tube with a vadose trench incised below: Pisa Passage, Shatter Cave.
Photo: A.P. Glanville

2. Waggon and Horses (ST 650456)
From this pub, situated on the Silurian rocks, an excellent view of the eastern Mendips and the surrounding area can be seen. To the south-east the Cretaceous Chalk and Greensand scarps may be seen in the distance. Both the Chalk and the Greensand once buried the Mendip area, but have now been eroded away.

3. Midway and Withybrook Slockers (ST 651469 and ST 655471)
Developed close to the limestone-shale boundary, Midway Slocker lies in the back garden of the house on the west side of the road and takes quite a large stream which resurges at both Ashwick Grove Lower Rising and St. Dunstan's Well. Withybrook Slocker is located further down the hill on the line of the Withybrook Fault and lies only a short distance away from the upstream limit of Withyhill Cave, one of the truncated passages in Fairy Cave Quarry. The water resurges at St. Dunstan's Well.

4. Ashwick Grove Valley (ST 648478)
This pleasant deep valley incised into the northern flank of Beacon Hill contains four springs. The highest of these, Ashwick Grove Higher Rising, yields over 1.5 million gallons of water derived from several of the multifarious swallets to the south of the Stoke St. Michael-Oakhill Road. Further down the valley are Ashwick Grove Middle and Lower Risings. Between them these two yield over three million gallons of water per day, part of which was used to power the now ruined mill further down the valley. Flow through times from sink to resurgences are very rapid and all three springs are prone to pollution from farm effluent and sewage. Several small caves can be seen in the valley sides but none extend very far.

5. Fairy Cave Quarry (ST 656477)

Although now disused, Fairy Cave Quarry is closed to visitors but it is a superb example, from an environmental point of view, of where not to quarry. Situated almost directly behind a major spring, the quarry during its life intersected over 25 caves; fragments of two major conduits which both drained to St Dunstan's Well. Over 4.5 km of passage has been recorded, of which 800 m have been quarried away. The western branch (Withyhill, Hillwithy and Hillier's Caves) is largely abandoned by its stream and until it was intersected by quarrying, extended almost the whole distance from the sink at Withybrook Slocker to the resurgence at St. Dunstan's Well. The eastern side (Balch, Fairy & Shatter Caves) is predominantly developed along the Withybrook fault. Many of the caves contain profuse stalagmite formations, including some of the best formations in Britain. The quarry nicely displays the steep dip of the limestone.

6. St. Dunstan's Well and Cave (ST 659479)

The large spring issuing from the base of the hill is St. Dunstan's Well. It is a composite spring with distinct east and west sides, both independently draining water from the 'slockers' to the south. Slocker is the eastern Mendip term for a swallet or stream sink. Proven feeders include Stoke Lane Slocker, and the Fairy Cave Quarry system, merging only at the spring itself. A few metres above the spring is an abandoned resurgence cave, St. Dunstan's Well Cave, which offers 120 m of arduous passage leading to a sump.

7. Browne's Grotto and Hole (ST 669476)

Both these caves represent truncated abandoned phreatic fragments of the same cave. The lower cave, Browne's Hole, begins as a roomy 2.5 m high phreatic tube. It was dug open in 1946 and yielded a human skeleton and other bones including a hyena tooth. The cave extends for some 300 m beyond the entrance chambers, as a series of low grovels. The quarries immediately down valley provide excellent exposures of the steeply dipping limestone and include a few minor caves. The bedding plane and joint control of the quarry faces and the cave remnants is clearly seen.

8. Stoke Lane Slocker (ST 669474)

Further up the valley, Stoke Lane Slocker is the sink for Mendip's largest swallet stream and the longest cave on East Mendip. Beyond the very aquatic entrance lies 2.2 km of passage, much of which is the gently graded streamway punctuated by eight sumps. The stream contributes some 75% of the water resurging at St. Dunstan's Well. Above the streamway are several very well decorated chambers. The poorly incised nature of the stream sink may suggest a relatively recent origin for the swallet cave, although the high level chambers are probably much older. The original sink may have been further upstream, closer to the shale-limestone boundary in Stoke St. Michael. The valley downstream is a good example of a dry valley.

SUGGESTIONS FOR FURTHER READING

The excursions in this guide are specific to the sites and features of the Mendip Hills, but the basic geomorphological and geological observations are applicable to other karst areas. For those wishing to discover more, there are several excellent introductory texts. These range from largely descriptive caving guidebooks through to more general texts on karst geomorphology. There is also a wealth of more specialised literature in caving club and academic journals. Detailed surveys of many of the cave systems are also available, often via caving shops or specific caving clubs (see the address for the National Caving Association).

Barrington, N. and Stanton, W.I. 1977. *The Complete Caves of Mendip and a View of the Hills*; Cheddar Valley Press, 234 pp. A very thorough guidebook, indispensable for anyone interested in Mendip caves and the karst landscape.

Duff, K.L. *et al.* 1985. *New Sites for Old*; Nature Conservancy Council. 192 pp. Details sites of geological interest in east Mendip.

Ford, D.C. and Williams, P.W. 1989. *Karst Geomorphology and Hydrology*. Unwin Hyman, London. A more specialist academic textbook.

Hanwell, J.D. and Newson, M.D. 1970. *The Great Storms and Floods of July 1968 on Mendip*. Wessex Cave Club Occasional Paper, Series 2, No. 2. Describes the events and aftermath of the 1968 floods.

Irwin, D.J. and Jarratt, A. 1999. *Mendip Underground; a cavers guide*. This is a specialist guidebook for cavers, describing the all the major caves on Mendip.

Lowe, D., and Waltham, A. 1995. *A Dictionary of Karst and Caves*. BCRA Cave Studies series No. 6. A useful non-specialist source of information on karst terminology.

Smith, D.I. (ed.) 1975. *Limestones and Caves of the Mendip Hills*. David and Charles, Newton Abbott. Although seriously in need of revision, this book provides a useful, if a little out of date, study of the Mendip karst.

Waltham, A.C., Simms, M.J. Farrant, A.R. and Goldie, H.S. 1997. *Karst and Caves of Great Britain*; Geological Conservation Review Series No. 12. Chapman and Hall. Documents all the sites of national importance in Britain, including many in the Mendip Hills.

Proceedings of the University of Bristol Spelaeological Society. These contain numerous papers on all aspects of cave and karst geomorphology and archaeology on the Mendips and elsewhere. Available from the Society (c/o Students Union, Queens Road, Bristol, BS8 1LN).

Proceedings of the Bristol Naturalists Society, Special Issue. No. 4. 1997. *The Mendip Hills*. Reprinted from Volume 55 (for 1995). Contains several papers on the geology and geomorphology of the Mendips.